A True Book

MERCURY

By Dennis B. Fradin

CHILDRENS PRESS®
CHICAGO

A *Mariner 10* photograph
of Mercury's surface

PHOTO CREDITS

The Bettmann Archive—15 (2 photos), 19, 23 (2 photos)

NASA—2, 11 (top left & bottom right), 20 (left), 29, 30, 33, 34 (right), 35, 38, 44 (left)

NASA-Jet Propulsion Lab—20 (right), 25, 43 (right), 45

North Wind Picture Archives—17

James Oberg—26 (left)

Photri—Cover, 4, 6, 7, 8, 10 (2 photos), 11 (top right & bottom left), 12, 13, 26 (right), 37, 40

UPI/Bettmann Newsphotos—34 (left), 44 (right)

Art by Len W. Meents—43 (left)

Cover—Mercury shot by *Mariner 10* on March 29, 1974

For Jeremy Newman

Library of Congress Cataloging-in-Publication Data

Fradin, Dennis B.
    Mercury / by Dennis B. Fradin.
        p.   cm. — (A New true book)
    Includes index.
    Summary: Describes the planet Mercury and humanity's search for knowledge about its nature.
        ISBN 0-516-01186-3
    1. Mercury (Planet)—Juvenile literature.
[1. Mercury (Planet)]   I. Title.
QB611.F73 1990   89-25359
523.4'1—dc20   CIP
                                       AC

TABLE OF CONTENTS

THE SOLAR SYSTEM

On a clear night, you can see many twinkling points of light in the sky. These are called stars. They look small because they are so far away. In fact, stars are giant balls of glowing, hot gas. There are many, many millions of stars in space. If you lived for a million years, you couldn't count them all.

Of all those stars, only one looks larger than a point of

Opposite page: Stars in the southern Milky Way

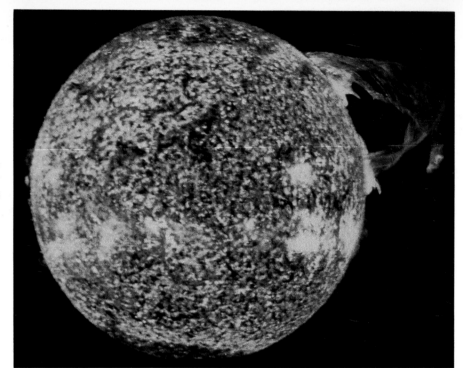

Close-up of the Sun, the star closest to the Earth

light to us. Only one can be seen in the daytime. We call that star the Sun. The Sun is just an average star in size and brightness. It seems bigger and brighter than the other stars because it is so much closer to us.

ORBITS OF THE PLANETS

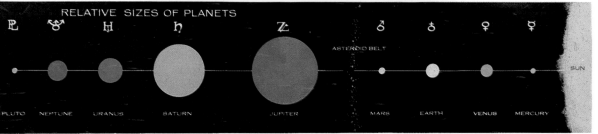

RELATIVE SIZES OF PLANETS

PLUTO NEPTUNE URANUS SATURN JUPITER ASTEROID BELT MARS EARTH VENUS MERCURY SUN

Nine planets are known to move around the Sun.

Planets are large objects that move around stars. Only one star is close enough for us to study its planets in detail. Again, that star is the Sun. Nine planets orbit the Sun. Mercury is the closest planet to the Sun. After Mercury come Venus, Earth, Mars, Jupiter, Saturn, Uranus, Neptune, and Pluto.

PLUTO
NEPTUNE
URANUS
SATURN
ASTEROIDS
SUN SPOTS
MERCURY
VENUS
EARTH
MARS
MOON
JUPITER

The Sun and its planets
are the main members of the
Solar System. The Solar
System can be thought of as
the Sun's family of heavenly
bodies. Moons—smaller
objects that orbit most of the
planets—are also part of the
Solar System.

SPOTTING MERCURY AND THE OTHER PLANETS

There are ways to tell
whether an object that we
see in the sky is a star
or a planet. For one thing,
stars seem to twinkle, or
flicker. This is because
Earth's air interferes with
the small point of light
that comes from a
faraway star.

Artist's painting of Pluto and its moon Charon (left).
Pluto and Neptune (right) are the farthest planets from the Sun.

But the planets are
closer to Earth, so the
disk of light from them
is larger. Planets do
not twinkle because the
Earth's air has less effect
on the way we see a
larger disk of light.

Uranus, Neptune, and

Saturn (top left),
Venus (above),
Jupiter (left), and
the red surface
of Mars (far left)

Pluto—the farthest planets
from the Sun—cannot be
seen by our eyes alone.
They are too far away. The
other six planets can

11

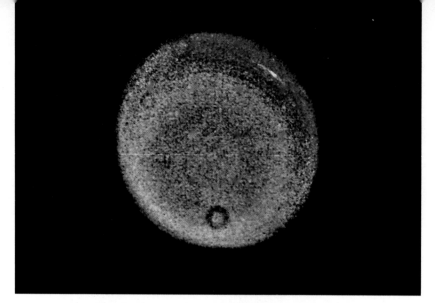

A *Voyager* spacecraft took this special photograph of Uranus.

be seen by the naked eye.
Mars can be spotted by
its red color. Brilliant white
Venus often appears after
sunset or before sunrise.
Jupiter and Saturn are
bright yellow-white planets.

   To see our planet Earth,
just look down at the ground!

View of Mercury from *Mariner 10*

   Mercury, the closest
planet to the Sun, is hard
to see. But Mercury isn't
dim. When visible, it is a
bright orange-yellow. It is
Mercury's size and location
that make it difficult to find.

Mercury is so small and so near the Sun that it is often lost in the Sun's glare.

Mercury can be seen only about 35 days a year. Some of that time it appears near the Sun just after sunset. You need a clear western horizon to find it then. Other times it appears in the east just before sunrise. You need a clear eastern horizon to spot Mercury at those times.

In ancient times (above) and in the Middle Ages (left) astronomers used simple instruments to study the heavens.

MERCURY AND ANCIENT PEOPLE

Ancient people thought there were only five planets—Mercury, Venus, Mars, Jupiter, and Saturn. They did not know that our Earth is also a planet.

15

Uranus, Neptune, and Pluto were not found until after telescopes were invented.

To the ancients, the planets were gods. The Babylonians called Mercury Nabou, the Ruler of the Universe. Nabou was the only one who could awaken the Sun and make it move across the sky. To the ancient Egyptians, Mercury was the god Sobkou.

The ancient Romans gave us most of the names we use for the planets today.

The Romans had a god named Mercury, who carried messages for the other gods. Mercury flew very fast. When the Romans saw a fast-moving planet, they named it Mercury, too. A substance used in thermometers is also called *mercury*. It was given that name because it moves fast, like the Roman god and the planet.

The Roman god Mercury

THE LENGTH OF MERCURY'S YEAR

Before telescopes were invented, little was known about the planet Mercury.

One of the few known facts about Mercury was the length of its year. The Polish astronomer Nicolaus Copernicus (1473-1543) figured that out. Mercury's year is 88 earth-days long. In other words, Mercury takes 88 earth-days to go around the Sun.

Mercury has the shortest

Nicolaus Copernicus discovered that the planets travel around the Sun.

year of any of the Sun's nine planets. This occurs because, as the Sun's closest planet, Mercury moves faster than the other planets and has the shortest distance to travel. Earth's year is about 365 days long—about four times as long as Mercury's.

Jupiter and four of its moons (left); Saturn's rings (right)

MERCURY THROUGH THE TELESCOPE

The first telescopes were built in the early 1600s. Telescopes gave astronomers closer views of the planets. Saturn was seen to have rings. Jupiter was seen to have moons orbiting it.

Astronomers found that Mercury goes through phases, or changes, like our Moon. In other words, different parts of Mercury are sunlit at different times. This occurs because Mercury is closer to the Sun than Earth is. We see different parts of Mercury's sunlit side as the angle between Earth, Mercury, and the Sun changes. The planet Venus also goes through phases.

Astronomers could not see much on Mercury, though, even with their telescopes. For one thing, Mercury is a small planet. Second, Mercury never appears high in the night sky, where planets are viewed best. It is always down low, where planets seen through telescopes look fuzzy due to Earth's air.

Several giant telescopes were built in the early 1900s. Astronomers hoped that these telescopes would show many more details on Mercury. They didn't. In fact, astronomy books published before the late 1970s are short on facts or contain wrong data about Mercury.

In the early 1900s, astronomers used telescopes such as these to study Mercury.

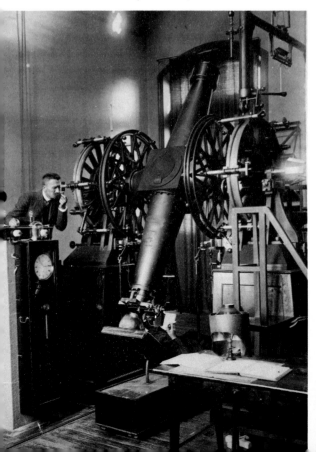

THE LENGTH OF MERCURY'S DAY

The length of a planet's day is the time it takes to spin once. Earth spins once every 24 hours. That means a day on Earth is 24 hours long.

Astronomers tried to find markings on Mercury. By watching markings, they could figure how long Mercury took to spin. But

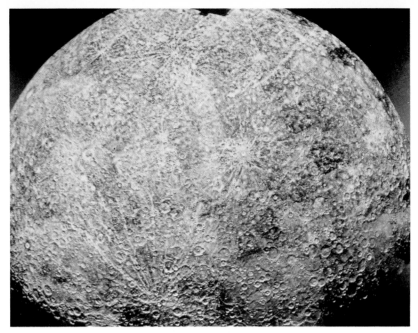

The surface markings seen in this close-up photograph of Mercury are not visible through a telescope.

astronomers had trouble finding such markings on Mercury with telescopes.

In 1965, radar solved the problem. Radar works by bouncing radio waves off an object. Using radar, scientists learned that Mercury's day is 59 earth-days long.

MARINER 10
VISITS MERCURY

The space age began in 1957, when the Soviet Union (USSR) launched the first artificial satellite. In 1969, the United States sent the first people to the Moon.

Sputnik (left) was the first artificial satellite.
American astronaut Edwin Aldrin (right) walks on the Moon.

The planets were too far away for people to visit as yet. Instead, the United States and the USSR sent spacecraft called space probes. These probes carry cameras and instruments but no people. The space probes send pictures and data back to Earth.

On November 3, 1973, the *Mariner 10* probe blasted off from Florida. Its first goal was to study Venus. Then it was to head toward its main target—Mercury.

Many things went wrong with this mission. It looked as if it would fail. But even though *Mariner 10* was out in space, scientists on Earth were able to fix the probe's problems by remote control.

Mariner 10 took several thousand pictures of Venus. The probe sent back information about Venus's atmosphere. Then it moved toward Mercury, the closest planet to the Sun.

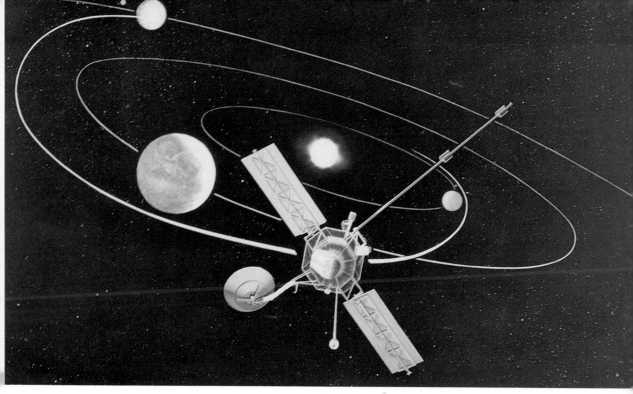

Drawing shows the path *Mariner 10* took on its voyage to Mercury.

Three different times
between March 1974 and
March 1975, *Mariner 10*
zoomed past Mercury. At its
closest, it came within 500
miles of Mercury. In addition
to taking thousands of

29

Mercury's heavily cratered surface was photographed by *Mariner 10*.

pictures of Mercury, *Mariner 10*
made thousands of
measurements of the planet.
Mariner 10 taught us more
about Mercury in a single
year than had been learned
in 5,000 years!

WHAT WE KNOW ABOUT MERCURY

Astronomers now have a fairly good picture of Mercury. Some of the information came from astronomers working on Earth. But most of it came from *Mariner 10*.

Mercury is the second-smallest planet. Only Pluto is smaller. Mercury's diameter is just 3,031 miles. Mercury would fit inside our Earth— the fifth largest planet— almost 10 times.

The force that pulls things toward a planet is called gravity. If Earth had no gravity, we could jump in the air and never come down. The smaller the planet, the weaker its gravity. Jupiter is much bigger than Earth, so it has stronger gravity. Mercury is much smaller than Earth, so it has weaker gravity.

If you weigh 80 pounds on Earth, you would weigh 30 pounds on Mercury, due to its lesser gravity. You could jump very high on Mercury.

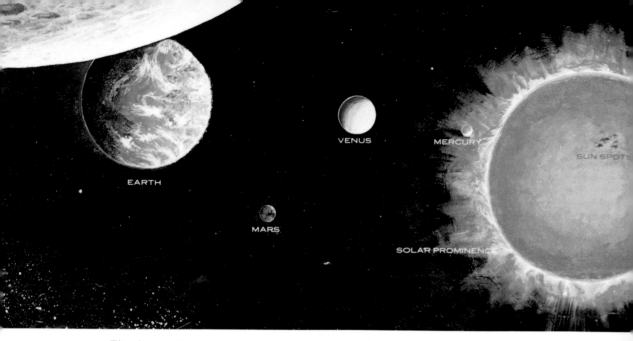

The inner Solar System, looking toward the Sun from Earth's Moon (top left).

You could throw a ball very far on Mercury.

You would need a spacesuit if you visited Mercury. For one thing, Mercury lacks the oxygen that human beings need to breathe. Also, Mercury's temperatures would kill a person without a spacesuit. Temperatures on Mercury reach about 800° F—hotter than an oven. But Mercury's night side has a low of about minus 300° F—much colder than temperatures at Earth's North Pole. Mercury also lacks the water that people need to drink.

Pictures sent to Earth by

"Earth-rise" as seen from the Moon (right).
Like our Moon, Mercury (left) is dry and covered with craters.

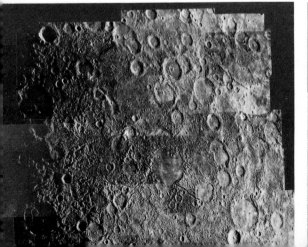
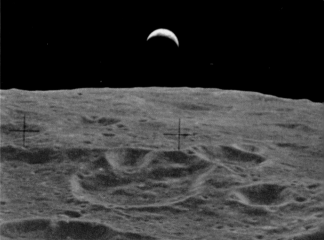

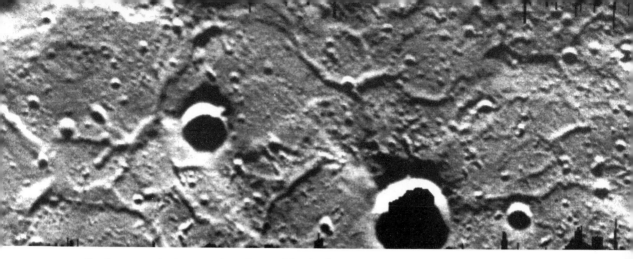

Craters are holes made when objects from space crash onto a heavenly body.

Mariner 10 showed that Mercury resembles Earth's Moon. Like the Moon, Mercury has millions of craters (holes) on its surface. Its largest known crater, the Caloris Basin, is about 800 miles in diameter. The smallest craters *Mariner 10* photographed are just several hundred feet in diameter.

Many of the craters may have been formed by meteoroids that struck Mercury. Meteoroids are pieces of stone and metal in the Solar System.

Meteoroids approach the Earth, too, but most of them burn up in our air. We see them as flashes of light called meteors. Mercury has no air, so meteoroids do not burn up when nearing the planet. Instead, they crash into the planet and make craters.

Comet Kohoutek visited the Solar System in 1974.

Perhaps comets (objects made of ice, gases, and dust) made some of the craters.

Mariner 10 also showed that Mercury has cliffs up to two miles high. The planet has hills and broad, flat areas called plains. The

The surface of Mercury from a distance of about 10,000 miles

plains seem to be covered
with lava like the lava that
comes from Earth's volcanoes.
No volcano has been seen to
erupt on Mercury, however.
The lava may have poured
out from inside Mercury
billions of years ago.

Seven of the nine planets in the Solar System have moons that orbit them. Earth has one Moon. Saturn has over 20 moons. Mercury and Venus are the only planets without moons.

Even with no moons, Mercury's sky is lovely. The Sun looks about 2½ times as big from Mercury as it does from Earth. But since Mercury has no air, its sky is black even when the Sun is up. Stars are visible there even in the daytime.

To astronomers, our Solar System is still a mystery.

MERCURY STILL HAS MANY MYSTERIES

Astronomers still have many questions about Mercury. Five billion years ago, the Solar System may have started as a cloud of dust and gas. The central part of the cloud may have become the Sun. The swirling pieces around the Sun may have joined to form larger and larger objects that became the planets.

There may have been some leftover pieces that did not go into the planets. Some of these leftovers may have later smashed into the planets. Were some of Mercury's craters made by these leftover pieces? Or were they all made by meteoroids and comets?

Why is Mercury so small?

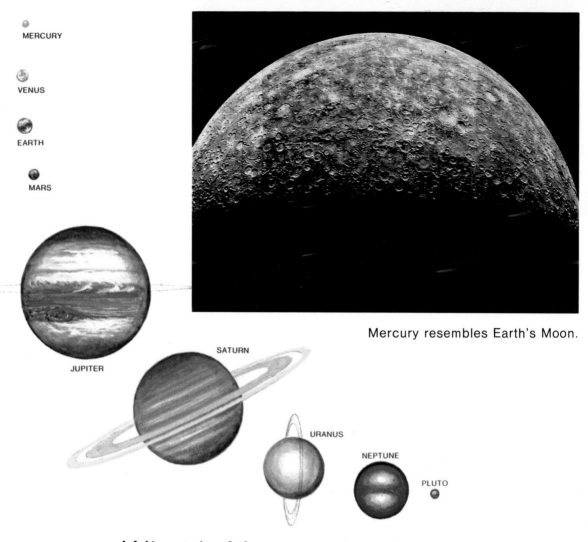

MERCURY

VENUS

EARTH

MARS

JUPITER

SATURN

URANUS

NEPTUNE

PLUTO

Mercury resembles Earth's Moon.

What is Mercury made of? What is it like inside the planet?

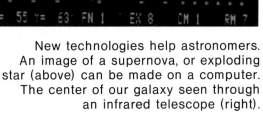

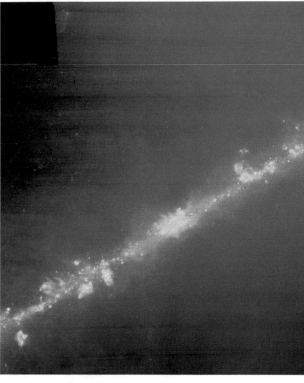

New technologies help astronomers.
An image of a supernova, or exploding
star (above) can be made on a computer.
The center of our galaxy seen through
an infrared telescope (right).

The answers to these
questions could do more
than just give us information
about Mercury. They could
help us better understand
how the whole Solar System,

including our Earth, was
formed. That is why we must
one day send more space
probes to explore Mercury,
the closest planet to the Sun.

FACTS ABOUT
MERCURY

Average Distance from Sun—
36 million miles

Closest Approach to Earth—
57 million miles

*Diameter—*3,031 miles

*Length of Day—*59 earth-days

*Length of Year—*88 earth-days

*High Temperature—*About
800° F

*Low Temperature—*About
-300° F

*Atmosphere—*Amost none

*Number of Moons—*0

*Weight of an Object on
Mercury That Would Weigh
100 Pounds on Earth—*
37 pounds

*Average Speed as Mercury
Orbits the Sun—*About
30 miles per second

WORDS YOU SHOULD KNOW

ancient(AIN • shent) —very old

astronomer(ast • RAH • nih • mer) —a person who studies stars, planets, and other heavenly bodies

atmosphere(AT • muss • feer) —the gases surrounding some heavenly bodies

billion(BILL • yun) —a thousand million (1,000,000,000)

Caloris Basin(kuh • LOR • uss BAY • sin) —the largest known crater on Mercury

comets(KAH • mets) —objects (made of ice, gases, and dust) that have long, glowing tails when near the Sun

craters(KRAY • terz) —holes that in many cases were made on a heavenly body by objects from space

gravity(GRAV • ih • tee) —the force that pulls things toward a heavenly body

lava(LAH • vah) —hot rock that comes out of a volcano

Mariner 10(MAIR • in • er TEN) —a U.S. craft that was the first space probe to approach Mercury

Mercury(MER • kyoo • ree) — the closest planet to the Sun

meteoroids(ME • tee • er • oidz) — pieces of stone and metal in the Solar System

million(MIL • yun) — a thousand thousand (1,000,000)

moons(MOONZ) — natural objects that orbit most of the nine planets

orbit(OR • bit) — the path an object takes when it moves around another object

oxygen(AHX • ih • jin) — a gas we need to breathe

plains(PLAYNZ) — large, nearly flat pieces of land

planets(PLAN • its) — large objects that orbit stars; the Sun has nine planets

radar(RAY • dahr) — a device that finds objects by bouncing radio waves off them

Solar System(SO • ler SISS • tim) — the Sun and its family of objects

space probes(SPAISS PROHBZ) — unmanned spacecraft sent to study heavenly bodies

stars(STAHRZ) — giant balls of glowing, hot gas

Sun(SUN) — the yellow star that is the closest star to Earth

telescopes(TEL • ih • skohps) — instruments that make distant objects look closer

universe(YOO • nih • verse) — all of space and everything in it

volcano(vahl • KAIN • oh) — an opening in the ground through which lava and other materials erupt

INDEX

About the Author

Dennis B. Fradin attended Northwestern University on a partial creative scholarship and was graduated in 1967. His previous books include the Young People's Stories of Our States series for Childrens Press. In the True Book series Dennis has written about astronomy, farming, comets, archaeology, movies, space colonies, the space lab, explorers, and pioneers. He is married and the father of three children.